COLUMBIA AND BEYOND

BY FRANKLYN M. BRANLEY

COLUMBIA AND BEYOND
The Story of the Space Shuttle

PHILOMEL BOOKS
New York

The author and Philomel Books wish to thank the following institutions
whose photographs have been used in this book:

The National Aeronautics and Space Administration, pp. 8, 12-13, 14, 16,
17, 19, 22, 24, 25, 28, 50, 53, 54, 55, 56, 62-63, 81, 82
Rockwell International, Rocketdyne Division, p. 29
Rockwell International's Space Systems Group, pp. 30, 31, 32, 34, 36, 38, 39,
40, 41, 42, 44, 50, 66, 71, 74
ERNO, pp. 51, 52
Hamilton Standard Division of United Technologies Corporation, p. 49

Library of Congress Cataloging in Publication Data

Branley, Franklyn Mansfield, 1915-
Columbia and beyond.
SUMMARY: Discusses the space vehicle, "Columbia," the space laboratory, "Spacelab," and other
proposed space projects.
1. Reusable space vehicles—Juvenile literature.
2. Spacelab Project—Juvenile literature. [1. Reusable
space vehicles. 2. Spacelab Project. 3. Space vehicles.
4. Space stations.] I. Title.
TL795.5.B72   629.45'4   78-26891
ISBN-0-399-20844-5

Published by Philomel Books
a division of The Putnam Publishing Group
51 Madison Avenue
New York, New York 10010
Revised edition 1984.

To Peg

CONTENTS

With astronauts John W. Young and Robert L. Crippen at the controls, the spaceship Columbia clears the launching pad on its first historic flight into space.

1.

Columbia in Orbit

At 7:00 A.M. on April 12, 1981, Columbia blasted into space from Pad 39A at the Kennedy Space Center in Florida. Astronauts John W. Young and Robert L. Crippen were at the controls. Twelve minutes later, Columbia was in orbit around the Earth. The age of the space shuttle had begun.

On November 28, 1983, Columbia was space-borne once again. It was some 250 kilometers above Earth, streaking through space at a speed of 28 000 kilometers an hour. That was fast enough to keep it in orbit, and fast enough to go once around Earth in 110 minutes. Its payload was the Spacelab developed by the European Space Agency.

The ship was in space, well above Earth's atmosphere, for ten days. Crew and passengers were well, having recovered from occasional airsickness, the usual experience during the early hours of spaceflight. This was the latest of many space shuttle missions that had already been flown in the 1980's by Columbia and Challenger, its sister ship.

9

Columbia is a new kind of space vehicle—one of three major parts that make up a space shuttle. The main fuel tank is one part. The solid-rocket boosters that fire during takeoff make up the second part. The ship itself, which is called the orbiter, is the third part. (An illustration showing the parts of the space shuttle can be found on pages 12 and 13.) In this mission, the orbiter was named Columbia. It is three ships in one—a rocket, a spaceship, and an airplane.

At takeoff Columbia is a rocket. It is fired straight up from the launching pad. Once in orbit it becomes a spaceship. Then, when it returns to Earth, Columbia lands like a glider—a motorless airplane.

Like the shuttle on a loom for weaving cloth, the space shuttle moves back and forth. If Columbia went into space and came right back, it would truly be a shuttle. Since it stays in space for several days before it returns, Columbia is really a delayed shuttle. However, in future flights it may simply go into orbit, unload cargo, and return immediately to Earth.

Columbia enables us to explore space. But it does more than that. It is a working vehicle that makes it possible to use space in many ways. The ship is large enough to carry tons of equipment for conducting experiments. Many of the experiments test how to use weightlessness and the vacuum of space. On Earth, weight measures the force pulling you down—it is a measure of the force of gravity. In space there is no "down"—the force of gravity is canceled—so there is no weight. If you stood on a scale, the reading would be zero. Also, there is a nearly perfect vacuum in space. That means there is no air or any other gases. On Earth, air may cause an impurity in the making of delicate instruments, such as calculators. So the air has to be removed from the chambers where the parts are made; a vacuum has to be created. In space, the vacuum is there all the time—no effort is needed to make one. (In Chapter 3 there will be more about the experiments aboard Columbia.)

In the early days of space exploration, a vehicle was used only once. Nothing was recovered and used again—not the rocket engines or the fuel tanks or the spaceships. It was like flying an airplane from New York to London, and then throwing the airplane away. Unlike those first space vehicles, Columbia can be serviced and made ready to fly again.

After a mission, Columbia returns to Earth, and goes into the shop. In a few weeks it is ready for another space flight. The ship is so constructed that it can complete at least one hundred flights during its lifetime.

Anyone can buy passage aboard Columbia—not for themselves perhaps, but for their experiments. A container about the size of a shoe box carrying materials to be exposed to space conditions costs about three thousand dollars; larger containers (about the size of a bushel basket) cost ten thousand dollars. People from industry and government, doctors and other specialists who wish to experience space conditions may also have a ride aboard Columbia. Tickets cost about seventy thousand dollars, but even at that price they are hard to get. Missions for the immediate future have already been filled.

Columbia is not a huge ship but it is large enough to be fairly comfortable for the crew, the scientists and passengers who are aboard. It is 37.24 meters long. That is much smaller than a Boeing 747—the big airplane that flies in Earth's atmosphere. In fact, when the first orbiter was being tested, it was carried by a 747. The big ship and the orbiter made many piggyback flights. During these flights the orbiter had no engines of its own. The ship was clamped atop the 747 and so carried aloft. At a height of seven or eight kilometers, the orbiter detached from the 747. The crew flew the ship like a glider and landed it to test the controls and the best way to bring the ship in for a smooth landing.

Columbia has three sections. The forward or flight section is where the crew and passengers are located. The middle

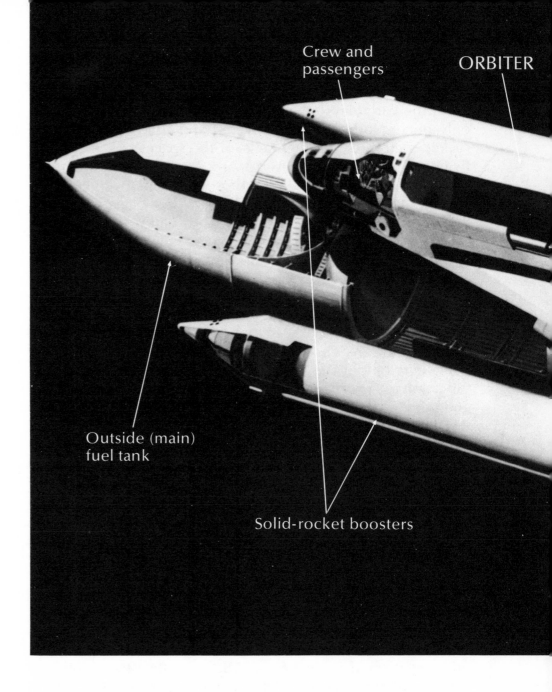

Crew and
passengers

ORBITER

Outside (main)
fuel tank

Solid-rocket boosters

section is called the cargo bay. This is where the payloads are.
A payload is what a spaceship carries into space. For instance,
a payload might include telescopes, satellites to be released or

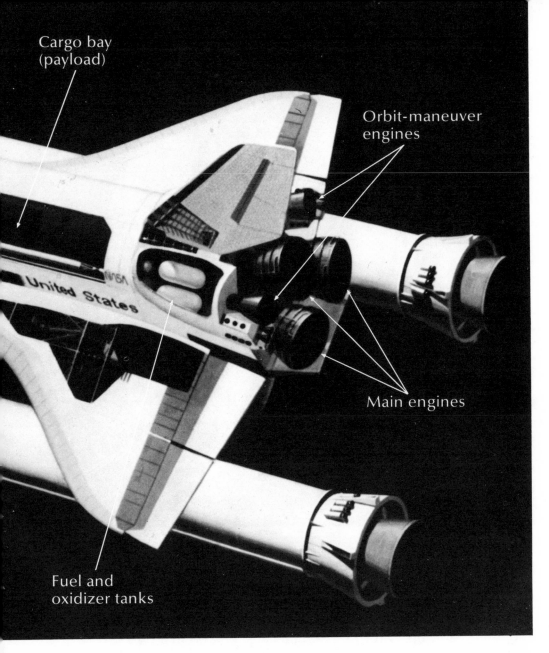

Cargo bay
(payload)

Orbit-maneuver
engines

Main engines

Fuel and
oxidizer tanks

The space shuttle has three parts:
the main fuel tank, the two
solid-rocket boosters, and the
orbiter. Shown here is the
orbiter named Columbia. At
launching Columbia rides atop
the main fuel tank.

equipment for experiments. Or a payload might be an entire
laboratory. There can be more than one payload aboard each
mission. The aft or rear section contains the main engines.

The flight section has seating for up to four crew members. The control panels in front of the crew are for flight. The panels behind are for the payload, and for docking with another ship. The panels to the side are for power and for communications within Columbia and from the ship to Earth station.

THE FLIGHT SECTION

Columbia is roomy enough to be quite comfortable. The three-person crew (in some missions there are four crew members) and up to four passengers are located in a two-level cabin at the front end of the ship. The upper level of the flight section is where the crew, consisting of mission commander, the captain of Columbia, and the payload specialist, who is responsible for the experiments, sit during takeoff. In front of the crew are the flight controls, which are the same

14

for each mission. Behind the crew are other panels of switches and controls. These may vary from one mission to another, since many of them are directly connected to the payload equipment. The controls move a loading arm that can lift an experiment out of the ship, or reach out into space to grasp a free-moving satellite and bring it into the cargo bay. Other controls in the flight section may regulate small engines that ease the ship to a docking with a satellite, or with another orbiter completing a rendezvous or link-up in space.

When the crew is in this forward section, they do not wear space suits. They work in a "shirt-sleeve" environment, that is, in conditions that are very much like those on Earth. The temperature stays between 16° and 30° C, and the air is kept at a comfortable humidity. Purifiers remove moisture from the air, carbon dioxide, and odors. Nitrogen and oxygen are measured, and quantities are added as needed.

In the lower level of the forward cabin are takeoff seats for the passengers. These people might be connected with the payload experiments, or they may be observers sent into space by their companies or governments to experience conditions there. Eventually, passengers aboard space shuttles may be tourists who are aboard just for an unusual vacation. This section of the cabin also has space for three "rescue" seats that can be set up for extra passengers in an emergency. It is possible that another ship may break down, or have an accident, and have to be abandoned in space. Should this happen, Columbia would rescue the crew and place them in these emergency seats for return to Earth.

This lower level also contains living quarters for the crew and passengers. These consist of areas for food preparation and serving, storage for personal items, and sleeping areas. The people aboard take turns sleeping. Sleeping in space is quite different from sleeping on Earth. On Earth, down is toward the center of Earth (the center of gravity), and up is away from the center. A person therefore lies down because

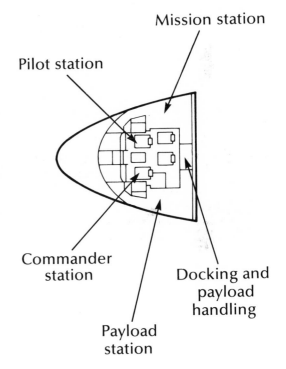

FLIGHT SECTION

Mission station

Pilot station

Commander station

Docking and payload handling

Payload station

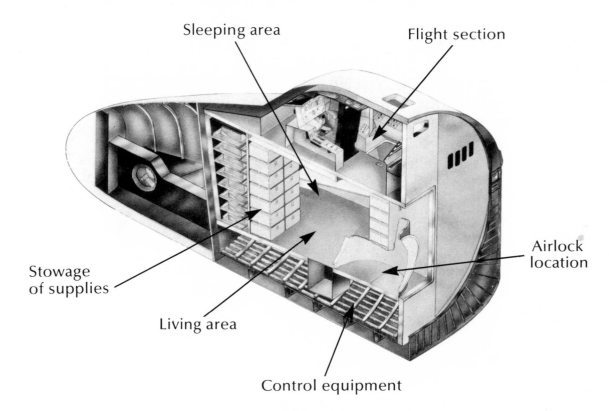

Sleeping area

Flight section

Stowage of supplies

Airlock location

Living area

Control equipment

The front section of Columbia is in three parts: the upper part is the flight section; the middle part is the living area; and the lower part contains equipment that controls conditions throughout the whole section.

he is pulled by gravity. In space, as has been explained, there is no pull due to gravity, so there is no down or up. Because of this, crew members in earlier spaceships found they could sleep while standing on their feet, or their heads, as well as lying "down" in the conventional way. In each case they had to be strapped in to keep from floating. Most people, however, found that they preferred to sleep lying down. It made them feel more as though they were in their familiar beds back home. The toilet is also here, as well as the wash-up center.

Going to the toilet is awkward. A person must hold on to handles to keep from floating. A man or a woman urinates into a funnel collector, either standing up or seated. A spring device fits the urinal funnel close to the body, so no liquid escapes. When in a seated position, the feet are put into loops and a belt is fastened around the waist. The toilet itself is connected to the waste-collecting system. It collects wastes from the people aboard, from wash water and from vomit bags, as well as gases from the storage of wet-waste materials.

Air and water are drawn into a unit that separates them. The air is filtered to remove odors, and returned to the cabin. Waste liquid is pumped to the waste-water storage tanks where it remains throughout the mission. Fecal wastes are dried in the toilet. Air used in the process is filtered and returned to the cabin. Liquids that are produced in the drying process go into the storage tanks. Solids, which have been dried and treated to kill germs, are stored in the waste collector for return to Earth. Vomit bags are made of material that allows air to pass through them. Their contents are also dried, and then stored in the same waste collector.

The galley is very compact. Water and food are stored here, as well as the microwave stove for preparing food. Be-

The four-person crew is having a meal in the living area. In the left foreground is the airlock which provides access to the cargo bay. The person at left is at the galley.

GALLEY DETAILS

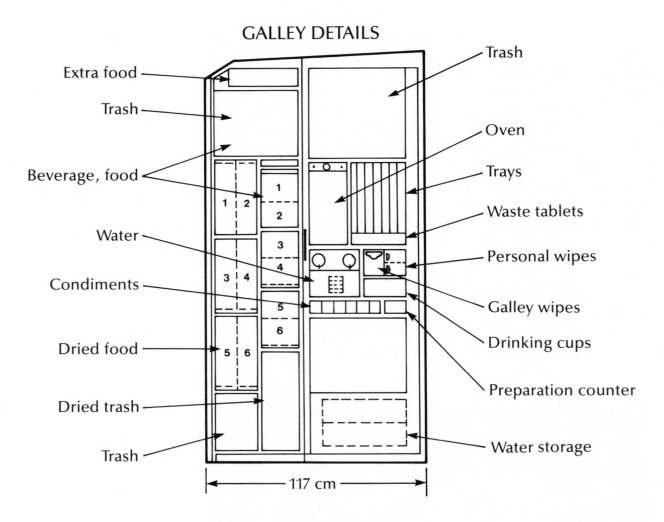

Extra food

Trash

Beverage, food

Water

Condiments

Dried food

Dried trash

Trash

Trash

Oven

Trays

Waste tablets

Personal wipes

Galley wipes

Drinking cups

Preparation counter

Water storage

117 cm

cause of tight storage space, most of the food is freeze-dried to concentrate it. Menus are varied, and the food is nourishing. However, hearty meals that include fresh food are not a part of space exploration. One must be careful when eating and drinking in space. Liquids are usually drunk out of squeeze bottles, water guns, or containers with straws in the lids. Liquids must not be set free. In zero gravity liquids form into drops that float about the cabin. The liquid could get into the wiring of the instruments and affect their operation. Also, when drops are very small, the liquid could be breathed into the lungs. Both possibilities must be avoided. Food must be prepared and handled carefully, so it is not set free to float inside the cabin.

There is no shower aboard Columbia because there is not enough room for one. The crew and passengers must settle for sponge baths. In future missions the arrangement of storage space and filtering equipment will probably be changed, so that showers can be installed. But bathing in space is not easy. As mentioned earlier, water tends to form into round drops that float. Therefore a person must get into a bag which keeps the drops from spreading into the cabin. One's head is outside the bag. A small amount of water is used to get wet, and then another small amount to rinse off—a person learns to bathe with no more than a pail of water. The waste water goes into the filtering system, and from there to the storage tanks to be used again. Most water aboard the ship is recycled.

The lower level of the forward cabin contains an airlock. This is a hatch, or door, through which a crew member crawls to go outside the ship or into the cargo bay. This operation is called EVA for extra (outside) vehicular activity.

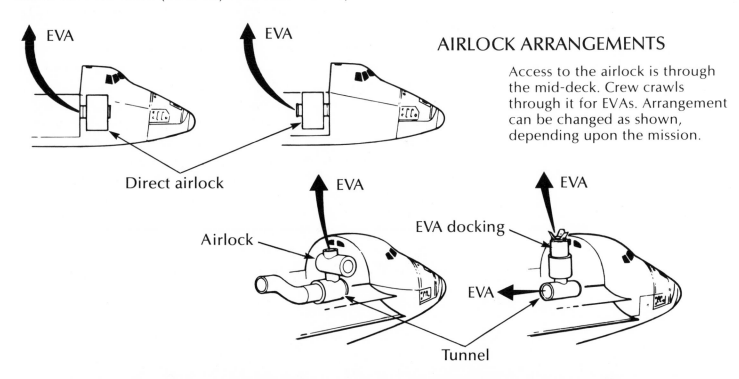

EVA

EVA

Direct airlock

AIRLOCK ARRANGEMENTS

Access to the airlock is through the mid-deck. Crew crawls through it for EVAs. Arrangement can be changed as shown, depending upon the mission.

EVA

Airlock

Tunnel

EVA docking

EVA

EVA

The lower part of the forward section contains pumps, filters, heaters, and coolers to regulate the air inside the entire section. Usually the crew does not have to reach this equipment. But should something go wrong, the area can be entered by removing panels in the floor.

Because of the limited storage space, not much food or other supplies can be stowed aboard Columbia. This limits the length of time that the crew and passengers can stay in orbit. The usual mission lasts seven days. But a mission might be extended to thirty days or more, if necessary. This can be done by using some of the payload space for storing food and water. Food, water, and oxygen are three requirements for staying alive; they must be carried aboard the ship. The fourth requirement is heat. There are heaters aboard, but heat is also available in space, for there is plenty of sunlight. In fact, cooling the ship is a bigger problem than heating it.

THE CARGO BAY

The cargo bay, the section that contains the payload, and which makes up the midsection of Columbia, is a huge area—18 meters long and 5 meters in diameter. Columbia can carry a payload of 29 484 kilograms. Hundreds of payloads will be carried into space. The forecast is that the space shuttle operation will last at least eleven years (1981-1992). During that time more than 570 missions will be flown, and each mission will carry one or more payloads. Very likely there will be several payloads aboard most missions since there is room in the cargo bay for them. On this mission Columbia contained only one—the European Space Laboratory, or Spacelab. (There will be more about the Spacelab in Chapter 3.)

Long doors run the full length of the cargo bay. When in orbit, the doors are usually opened wide. That permits the crew to work with the payload. This can be done either from inside the flight section, or by going outside to the cargo bay after putting on a space suit. Temperature regulators that are built into the doors operate only when the doors are open.

Heat that comes from body warmth, from cooking, and from control equipment builds up in the forward section where the crew and passengers are located. A plumbing system collects the heat and takes it to radiators fastened to the cargo-bay doors. From there the heat escapes into space. Ovens used for experiments in the payload also produce heat, more in some payloads than in others, depending upon the kind of equipment that is being used.

On this mission, the experiments and control equipment that are part of Spacelab created quite a lot of heat, but the lab had its own temperature-control devices. They held the temperature within the same boundaries as the rest of the ship, and so put no extra load on the cargo-bay radiators.

During takeoff and landing, the cargo-bay doors are closed. At these times the ship is cooled by systems that are very much like large refrigerators.

An important mechanism in the cargo-bay area is the payload handler. Behind the flight controls in the flight section there are banks of switches and dials that refer to the payload. The payload specialist moves a small regulator up, down, sideways, or whatever. A television screen shows the actual motions of the payload handler as it moves in the same way as the regulator.

On the 1983 mission there was not much need for the handler. It is, however, very useful for other activities that will be carried out by future orbiters. For example, some ships will launch satellites of various kinds. The payload handler will lift the satellite out of the cargo bay and move it overboard, free of the orbiter. The satellite can stay in the same orbit, or it could have its own engines. Those engines might send the satellite to a different elevation; or they might send it on a mission to another planet.

The payload handler can also pick up a satellite from out-

The payload handler lifts a satellite out of the cargo bay. Once the satellite is free, it may go into an orbit close to Earth. Or, it may have engines powerful enough to put it into an orbit that will take it to another planet.

side the ship and move it into the cargo bay. In this way, orbiters will be used as workshops for checking satellites; repairing them if necessary, and sending them back into orbit. The payload handler is, in effect, the crew's "hands," doing all sorts of jobs outside the flight section.

But on certain missions, crew members will have to go outside the flight section. They may have to repair satellites themselves (as shown in the illustration on page 49) or move equipment that is too far away to be reached by the payload handler. They may also have to make repairs on the orbiter itself. In certain situations, they may even have to go out into space—for instance, to rescue crews from other ships. To do any of these tasks, they will have to wear a space suit that contains EVA life-support equipment. This consists of oxygen to breathe, temperature and air-pressure controls, and filters to remove moisture and carbon dioxide. The suit also contains radios for sending and receiving. Should the crew member go beyond the ship, a line, called an umbilical, is needed. Otherwise, it is possible that the person would float away into space. The line is called an umbilical because it connects the ship and astronaut just as a mother and child are connected by an umbilical cord. Once suited, the astronaut crawls through the airlock connecting the flight section to the cargo bay. Two or sometimes three space suits are carried on each mission.

Space suits for the shuttle missions are more comfortable than the old ones that were used by the Apollo astronauts. They are lighter, and it's easier to move in them. The suits are more economical as they now come in small, medium, and large sizes, and so do not have to be made separately for each person. Also, they fit both men and women. Each suit comes in two sections—upper and lower—and each part is sealed so air cannot escape. The life-support equipment is contained in the backpack. A box in the chest section houses controls and a tiny computer that checks conditions in the suit, correcting

23

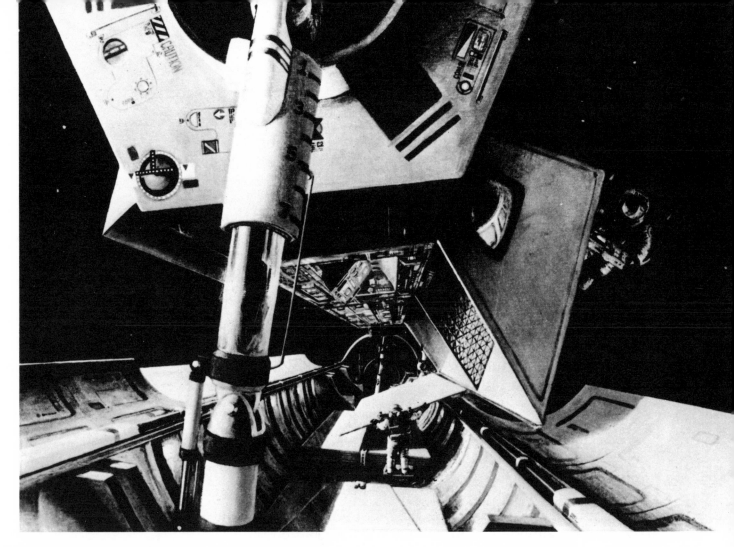

EVA for construction. Astronauts shift panels in the cargo bay. Another astronaut moves to the outer part of the module they are building. Small jets move him into position.

them as needed. Small jets built into the pack make it possible for the astronaut to move around in space. Controls for these jets are in the armrests that fold out of the way when the astronaut is working on a task. The only way to move in space other than holding onto the ship and pulling or pushing one's self is by ejecting a gas from these small jets. Gases escaping from these nozzles move the astronaut ahead, just as air escaping from a balloon pushes the balloon ahead.

Underwear that controls heat is worn under the space suit. It contains thin plastic tubing. Water that is kept moving

24

through the tubing picks up body heat. The water goes to the backpack where the heat radiates into space, keeping the astronaut at a comfortable temperature. Larger tubes that carry oxygen are also built into the garment. These absorb heat as well.

An orbiter may become disabled, and an emergency rescue may be necessary. Should that happen, the procedure is as follows. Two members of the crew wear space suits, but the commander and payload specialist are enclosed inside rescue balls. On this mission there are sufficient rescue balls for all passengers as well. An advantage to these balls is that, unlike

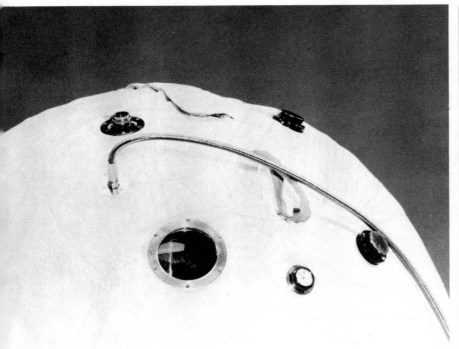
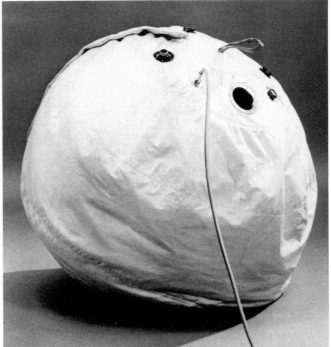

There is a connection, or umbilical, between the rescue ball and the ship. When a rescued crew member first enters the ball, the mother ship provides oxygen for breathing and communications through the umbilical. The ball becomes self-sustaining only after the umbilical is disconnected.

A RESCUE BALL

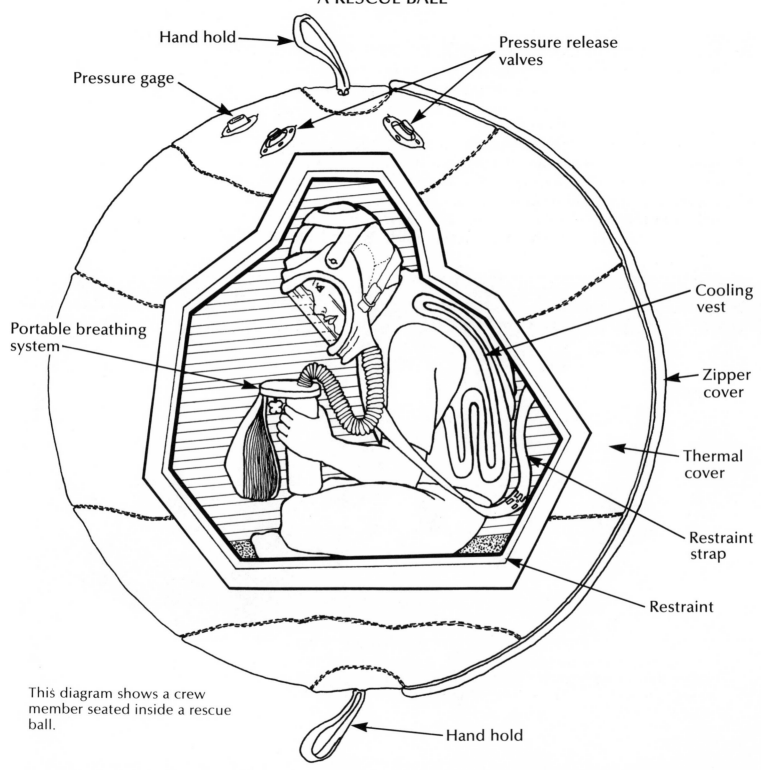

Hand hold

Pressure release valves

Pressure gage

Cooling vest

Zipper cover

Portable breathing system

Thermal cover

Restraint strap

Restraint

This diagram shows a crew member seated inside a rescue ball.

Hand hold

the space suits, they are small and compact. When inflated, a rescue ball is only 86.36 centimeters in diameter. It can be folded and stored within a standard shuttle locker—a space only 48 by 43 by 25 centimeters.

The rescue balls are designed to provide life support for one hour, which is ample time to complete an emergency transfer between space orbiters. The main parts of a rescue ball are the ball itself and a portable oxygen system. The ball is made of plastic material combined with nylon. Temperature control is provided by several layers of plastic coated with aluminum, enclosed within the inner wall of the ball. Inside the ball there is a mask that is connected to a portable breathing system. The person steps into the ball, which can then be zipped closed from either inside the ball or outside it. The ball is then inflated with gas from a small canister. After that it is kept inflated by using the exhaled gases from the breathing apparatus. The equipment has controls for regulating the flow of oxygen, and a device for absorbing carbon dioxide from exhaled breath.

Once inside the ball, a person has no freedom of action; the only contact with the outside world is visually through a small window. However, the stay inside is brief, since the balls can be transferred quickly to a rescue ship. To do this, the payload handler could be used. It would grasp the ball by a ring that is fastened to it, lift up the ball, and swing it over to the cargo bay of the rescue ship. Or the rings on the rescue balls might be clamped to hooks on a "clothesline" apparatus connecting the two ships and pulled along to the rescue vehicle. Should neither of these procedures work out, the balls could be carried by the people in space suits. It would be hard to carry them on Earth, because of their weight. But in space, where there is no weight because there is zero gravity, no effort is needed to pick up and carry a full-grown person— even a small child could do it. In fact, one would have to hold on to the ball, or it would float away.

Orbit-maneuver engines

Reaction-control engines

Main engines

This view of Columbia on landing approach shows the engines clearly.

ORBITER ENGINES

The rear part of the orbiter contains three main engines. In addition, this section contains smaller engines called reaction-control or thruster engines, and engines for turning the ship around.

28

The Main Engines

The three main engines are huge. Each is 4.3 meters long. The nozzle opening is very wide—2.4 meters across, so a lot of fuel can be burned in a very short period of time. Much more fuel is needed than can be contained aboard the orbiter, so most of the fuel is carried in a separate fuel tank—called the main tank or the external tank. The tank is 47 meters long, longer than Columbia; and 8.38 meters across. Total weight of the tank and its contents is over 743 thousand kilograms.

One of the three main engines being tested.

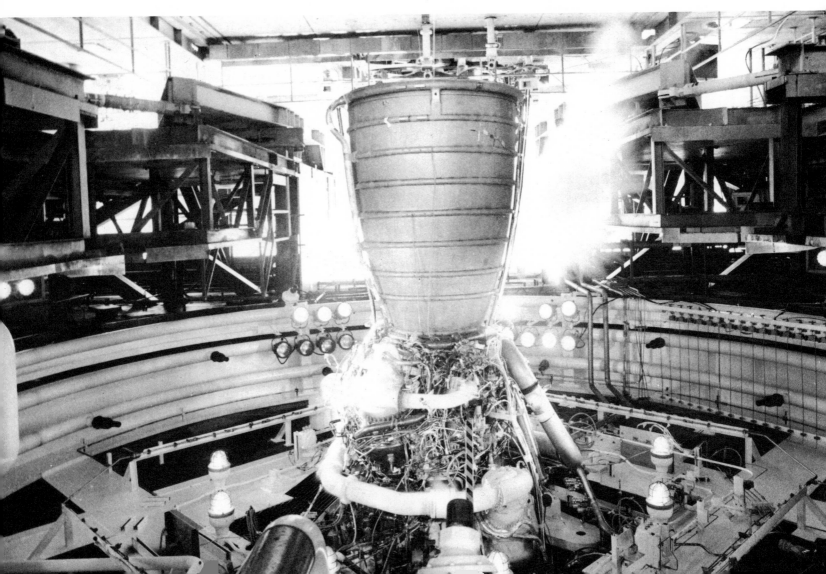

A liquid-oxygen tank is in the nose section, and it is separated from the liquid-hydrogen located in the rear section. The space between the two tanks contains the controls for mixing the fuel (the hydrogen) with the oxidizer (the oxygen), and the controls for regulating the flow.

The total burn time of all this fuel is eight minutes. During that time the engines burn over 500 thousand kilograms of liquid-oxygen and 100 thousand kilograms of liquid-hydrogen. These main engines, together with solid-rocket boosters, put the ship almost into orbit.

The main fuel tank, which supplies the three main engines. This tank is not reused. It is jettisoned eight minutes after takeoff.

THE MAIN OR EXTERNAL TANK

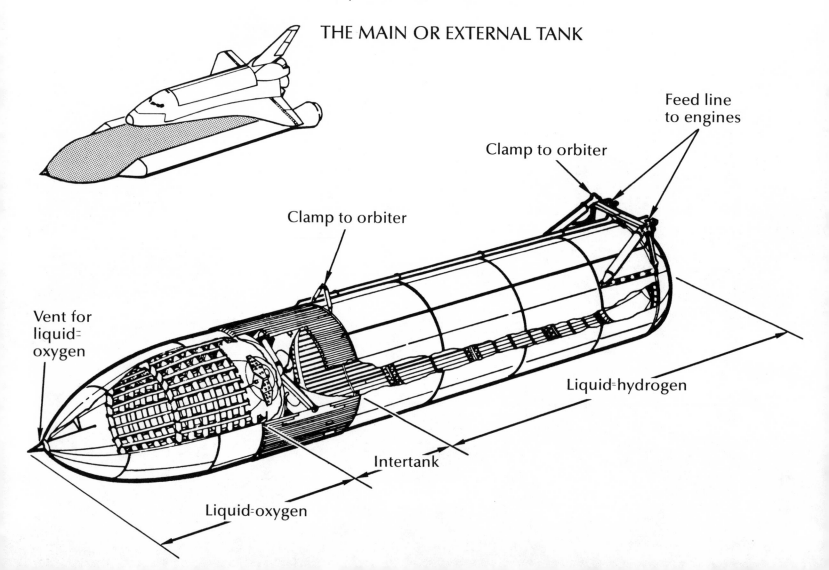

Feed line to engines

Clamp to orbiter

Clamp to orbiter

Vent for liquid-oxygen

Liquid-hydrogen

Intertank

Liquid-oxygen

The Solid-Rocket Boosters

The shuttle also contains solid-rocket booster engines, which provide extra thrust at takeoff. They are fastened to the main fuel tank. After the first two minutes of flight, these engines drop away. They are recovered, however, and used again.

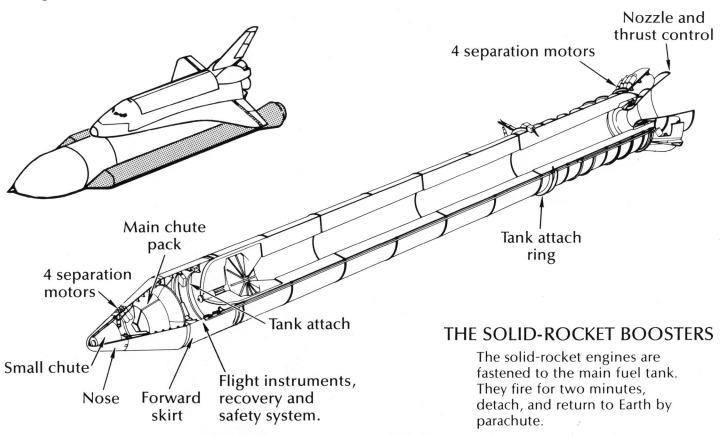

Nozzle and thrust control

4 separation motors

Main chute pack

Tank attach ring

4 separation motors

Tank attach

Small chute

Nose   Forward skirt   Flight instruments, recovery and safety system.

THE SOLID-ROCKET BOOSTERS

The solid-rocket engines are fastened to the main fuel tank. They fire for two minutes, detach, and return to Earth by parachute.

The fuel in these engines is mostly aluminum powder and iron oxide. After fifty-five seconds of firing full blast, the engines are throttled down. This eases the strain on the main fuel tank. But it still accelerates the shuttle, making it go faster.

As can be seen from the diagram on page 31, fuel makes up most of the boosters. Regulators, which control the rate of burning, and parachutes that lower the engines to the ocean are packed in the nose section. These take very little space.

Two minutes after takeoff, clamps that hold the boosters to the main tank are released. Small separation motors in the front and rear sections fire to move the boosters away from the shuttle. The nose cone is detached, and the first of the parachutes springs open.

Three larger chutes are pulled out by the small chute. They ease the boosters to a soft splashdown. After recovery, the boosters are serviced, recharged, and fastened to another shuttle to be used again.

THE ORBIT-MANEUVER ENGINES

Two orbit-maneuver engines are located in pods on either side of the main engines.

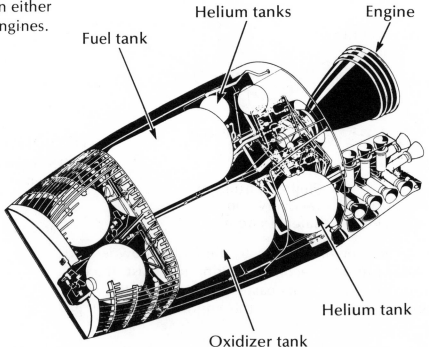

Fuel tank

Helium tanks

Engine

Helium tank

Oxidizer tank

The Orbit-Maneuver Engines

These engines are built into the orbiter itself. They are smaller than the main engines, and are used for the final boost into orbit. They also can change the ship's path once it has achieved orbit, so the ship can rendezvous with another ship or with a satellite. These engines slow the ship down so it can move out of orbit to begin the journey back to Earth.

Fuel and oxidizer are pushed to the engines. The fuel is monomethyl hydrazine, and the oxidizer is nitrogen tetroxide. When these two substances combine, they ignite and produce a hot gas that provides the thrust needed to propel the orbiter. Each engine is built to last at least one hundred missions.

The pods or bulges that house these engines also contain the fuel tanks. There is enough fuel in them to last through this particular mission. Other missions may require additional fuel. When needed, the extra fuel is stored in the rear section of the cargo bay in reserve tanks.

The Reaction-Control or Thruster Engines

The orbiter contains thirty-eight thruster engines, which do the main job of keeping the ship in even flight, and six smaller engines, which make fine corrections such as slight movements up, down, or sideways.

The thrusters are used to ease the ship into final orbit and to speed it up slightly if needed. But the main job of the thruster engines is to keep the ship from rolling, from pitching up and down, and from swinging from side to side. They hold the ship in steady and even flight.

Twenty-eight of these engines are in the pods that house the maneuvering engines. In addition, ten are located in the nose section of the ship, where the very small engines for fine corrections are also located. During return to Earth, the forward engines are shut down, and only the rear thrusters are used to keep the ship stable.

33

THE REACTION-CONTROL SYSTEM

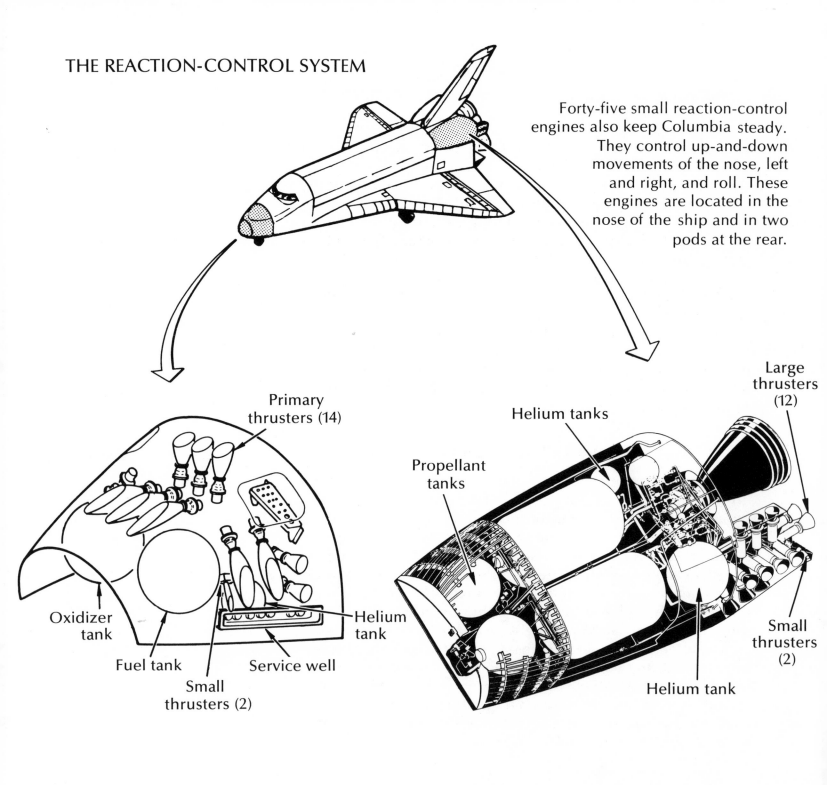

Forty-five small reaction-control engines also keep Columbia steady. They control up-and-down movements of the nose, left and right, and roll. These engines are located in the nose of the ship and in two pods at the rear.

Primary thrusters (14)

Oxidizer tank

Fuel tank

Small thrusters (2)

Service well

Helium tank

Helium tanks

Propellant tanks

Large thrusters (12)

Small thrusters (2)

Helium tank

The fuel used in the thrusters is the same as the fuel used in the maneuvering engines. It is hypergolic. That means that it ignites when the fuel (monomethyl hydrazine—MMH) and the oxidizer (nitrogen tetroxide—N_2O_4) join together. No spark is needed.

Information about the attitude of the ship—whether it is in even flight, or turning one way or the other—is fed into a small onboard computer. If correction is necessary, the computer figures out how to fix the situation. Signals then go out to the thruster engines, and they are turned on for the number of seconds, or fractions of seconds, needed to correct the condition.

HEAT CONTROL

During launch and reentry, parts of the shuttle become very hot. Friction with the outside air creates heat. The entire undersurface glows red, and the leading edges of the nose, wings, and tail become white-hot, as shown in the illustration on page 50. Columbia is heavily insulated to control the heat. If it weren't, the heat might spread to other parts of the ship, and possibly burn them out.

Much of the insulation is made of layers of glasslike bricks. They are not destroyed by the heat, and so can be used over and over again. The entire ship is insulated, some parts more heavily than others. The hottest regions, and the nose and leading edges of the wings, are covered with a carbon material that can withstand very high temperatures. Beneath this surface there is additional insulation to protect the interior of the ship.

During return to Earth, the insulation plus the cooling system keep the flight section at or below the allowed maximum temperature of 32° C.

Inside the assembly building at the Kennedy Space Center. The size of the men gives some indication of the size of the building. Columbia, the orbiter, will be mated to the main fuel tank and to the solid-rocket boosters.

2.

Columbia – From Takeoff to Orbit

A typical mission of Columbia starts three days before launch. A flight is in planning stages for years, and final preparations begin months earlier. The mission itself, the loading of crew and passengers, the fueling and firing of the engines, and insertion into orbit start at countdown.

Inside the large assembly building at the Kennedy Space Center, Columbia, the orbiter of the 1983 mission, was mated to the main fuel tank and to the two solid-rocket boosters. It was then a complete space shuttle, upright and pointing to the sky. Slowly, inch by inch, the entire shuttle was rolled to pad 39A, the takeoff site. For days, mechanics and engineers swarmed over the shuttle. Finally the payload was checked out, and all systems were OK. It was time for the crew to go aboard.

Columbia with its engines stands free on pad 39A. Cables (umbilicals) and catwalks extend to it from the support scaffold. Columbia and the platform were moved here along the tracks to the right.

All members of the crew, and the passengers, too, had to "lie" in the seats—nose up—just as the nose of the ship was up. It was awkward climbing into the seats, but comfortable enough once the straps were fastened down.

Fuel was pumped into the main tank. Then came the final countdown to ignition. The three main engines were firing full; then the boosters cut in.

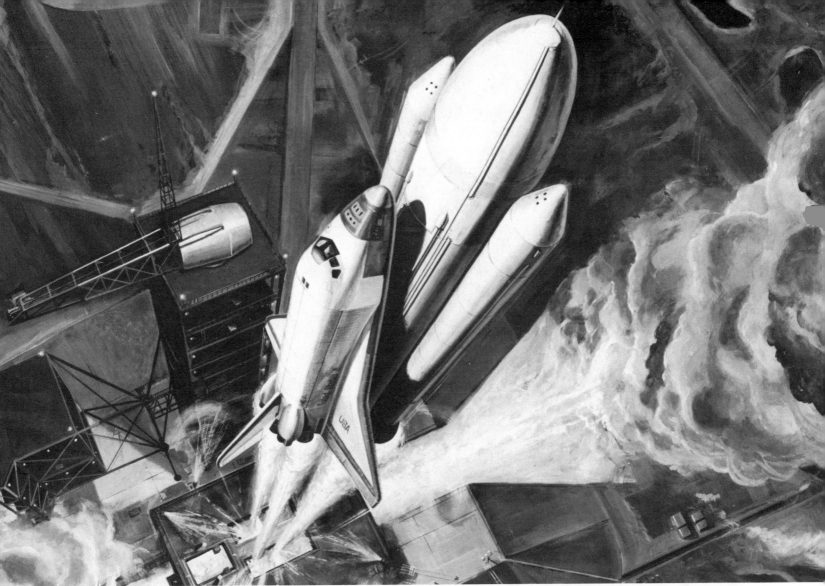

Cables connecting the shuttle to the launching tower dropped away as the engines fired. Hot gases roared into the concrete pit below the pad. At first the shuttle did not move. Then, ever so slowly, Columbia cleared the pad. It looked as if it were standing on a tower of flames. In seconds it took off, moving straight up and accelerating rapidly.

As pressure built up, the crew members were pushed hard

Moments after lift-off. All engines are firing full. Flames and hot gases pour into the cooling canyon. The gantry has swung out of the way. Columbia rises on a tower of flames. Total weight is 2 000 000 kilograms (4 500 000 pounds).

Space shuttle accelerates, and climbs through Earth's atmosphere. All engines are full on, for these are the moments when the greatest thrust is needed. Soon the solid rockets will cut back to reduce strain on the main fuel tank.

against their seats, just as you are when a car accelerates rapidly. But the pressure never reached more than three g's—three times the force of gravity. A person weighing 80 kilograms would be pushed against the seat with a force of 240 kilograms.

At lift-off all engines fired full on. After two minutes the solid-rocket boosters burned out. Altitude was a bit over 45

kilometers, and the shuttle was going almost 1 400 kilometers a second.

The solid rockets broke free of the main fuel tank. Small rockets in the nose and rear sections fired to push the boosters away and clear of Columbia. Moments later, the nose sections of these rockets were jettisoned (released), and small parachutes opened. These caught the air, the little there was at

Columbia, two minutes after launch. The main engines are full on. The solid-rocket boosters have detached, and small engines are firing to move the boosters away from Columbia.

that altitude, and pulled out the three main chutes. The burned-out rockets descended to the sea where they floated on the surface. Almost at once, a recovery ship lifted them out. The rockets were returned to Florida where they will be repaired, recharged, and made ready for another mission.

After eight minutes the main engines shut down. The fuel in the main tank was used up, and so the tank was released. Since there was no plan to reuse this tank, it was allowed to fall to Earth. Friction turned it white-hot, and most of it changed to gases. What solids were left fell into the lower Atlantic Ocean. The orbiter's altitude at that time was close to 240 kilometers, and its velocity more than 7 800 meters a second. A short burst of the maneuvering engines was all that was needed to put Columbia into its path around the Earth.

Ten minutes after lift-off Columbia was in orbit, sweeping all the way around the planet in less than two hours.

After eight minutes all the fuel is gone from the main tank. The tank is no longer needed; it separates from Columbia. The structures that connect the two can be seen below the tank. Columbia is free.

3.

Spacelab and the European Space Agency

The major working mission of Columbia was to carry Spacelab into orbit, and return it safely to Earth.

Spacelab was a self-contained laboratory located, as we have seen, in the cargo bay. It was complete with computers, recorders, measuring instruments, and equipment for conducting all sorts of experiments. There were seventy-five experiments included in this flight alone. An airlock connected Spacelab to the flight section. Both areas had controlled conditions, so the scientists worked in comfortable surroundings, like those on Earth.

In addition to the lab, there was a U-shaped aluminum platform that reached across the cargo bay. The pallet carried equipment that was exposed to outer space conditions when the top of the

43

EUROPEAN SPACE AGENCY'S SPACELAB

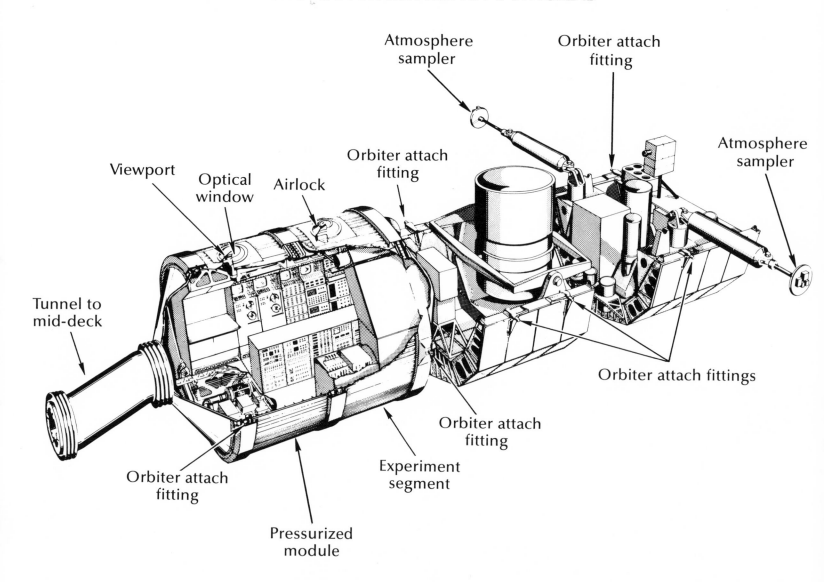

Details of ESA's Spacelab which will be flown on over 200 missions of the shuttle.

cargo bay was opened. The eighteen experiments aboard it used to advantage the high vacuum of outer space, the intense ultraviolet light, and other kinds of radiation such as X rays. Scientists also observed the effects of cosmic particles on the experiments. These are high energy particles that are smaller than atoms, and which move through space at high speeds.

On this flight one of the devices on the pallet was a telescope. Astronomers were using it to scan the sky without interference from Earth's atmosphere. (At 250 kilometers above the Earth, Columbia was well above the Earth's atmosphere, which extends to about 175 kilometers.) In particular, the astronomers on this mission were taking a close look at those stars that give off ultraviolet light in large amounts. Earth's atmosphere filters out most ultraviolet light, so these stars cannot be seen from the surface of the Earth. They were first sighted briefly by using telescopes aboard satellites that circled the Earth. They are intensely hot stars—much hotter than the sun—which give off tremendous amounts of energy.

The other platform contained cameras, antennas, and buckets for collecting samples of the molecules in space and in the outer atmosphere. This platform also contained furnaces for melting metals in zero gravity. The high temperatures necessary for this experiment are reached by concentrating solar energy. This was done with curved reflectors that focus a large amount of energy on a small container. Experiments in the platforms were conducted by controls inside Spacelab. Had it become necessary to check or adjust an experiment by hand on either of the platforms, a crew member could have put on a space suit and gone outside the Lab. Passage out of the Lab is through an airlock located in the ceiling.

There was quite a lot of room inside the Lab, so scientists could move about. Equipment and controls were clustered so they could be reached easily. Windows in the ceiling area allowed the scientists to watch for unexpected events that might occur—

the passage of a large meteoroid, for example, or a sudden explosion on the surface of the sun. Equipment storage, power supply, and controls for regulating temperature and air supply were located beneath the floor. To reach this area, floor panels could be lifted up. The racks of controls can be removed unit by unit for repair, or for exchange with different panels. Also, the equipment beneath the floor can be rolled out and replaced as needed. This is important, for Spacelab will be used over and over again for various kinds of study and research. It is planned that Spacelab will be the main payload on 226 of the 572 flights scheduled during the eleven-year shuttle program.

Spacelab was designed, built, and paid for by ESA—the European Space Agency. Countries that make up the agency are West Germany, Belgium, Denmark, France, Great Britain, the Netherlands, Italy, Sweden, Switzerland, and Spain. On this particular flight Japan and Austria also had experiments aboard.

Countries in the agency have been working together for many years on space-exploration projects. The largest contributors are France, Germany, Great Britain, and Italy. They have already developed and launched a communication satellite. Telephone calls are sent to it from one part of Europe, relayed back to another location, and then routed to the person being called. A large part of Europe's telephone and telegraph traffic goes by way of this satellite.

Additional satellites will be launched regularly. One of these will establish communication between all parts of Europe, Asia and Africa.

The ESA has also developed its own satellite launcher. This is a rocket that fires satellites from the northern coast of South America.

Each of the ESA countries built some part of the Lab. Then the main company, ERNO of West Germany, put it together. Each country has its own experiments aboard. The number of experiments per country is regulated by the country's share of the total cost. West Germany's share is more than 50 percent.

The Spacelab scientists are experimenting to find out how metals and glass behave in zero gravity and in a practically perfect vacuum. Here on Earth, metals and glass flow downward when heated because they are pulled by gravity. Since the heaviest part is pulled down the most, it is often difficult to produce metal or glass of exactly the same consistency throughout. It is hoped that it will be possible to do this in space. Also, it will be possible to produce perfect crystals of various salts when they are grown in a constant vacuum and in zero gravity. There are containers for growing crystals inside the Lab as well as outside where materials are exposed to all outer space conditions. There will be more about crystals in Chapter 5.

On Earth maintaining a high vacuum is an expensive part of processing materials for electronics, medicine, and biology. In space, no effort is needed because there is no air; in fact, outer space is an almost perfect natural vacuum. Very likely the experiments will show that delicate parts for computers and regulators for treatment of various ailments should be made in space.

Biologists in Spacelabs will continue to test the growth of bacteria and of all kinds of plants, the germination of seeds, the growth of roots and leaf structures. Do roots grow "down" when there is no down? Will trees grow horizontally rather than vertically? Is there a limit to the size of a plant that grows in zero gravity? Why do plants as we know them on Earth stop growing when they reach a certain size? Perhaps gravity is a factor since it affects the transfer of liquids in a plant. In order for liquids to reach the top of a tree, they must counteract gravity which tends to pull them down. Without the force of gravity plants may just keep on growing forever.

Cameras and measuring instruments are aimed at Earth to survey the planet. They look for deposits of raw materials—for example, clues to deposits of coal and oil. They survey crops

(opposite)
Interior of Spacelab, showing
arrangement of panels, and the
space available for scientists to
move about in. Notice the
entrance to tunnel connecting
with mid-deck of the flight
section. Airlock for possible EVA
is at the top.

During reentry, friction with
Earth's atmosphere heats the
ship. The nose and edges of the
wings are white-hot, and the
bottom of the ship glows red.

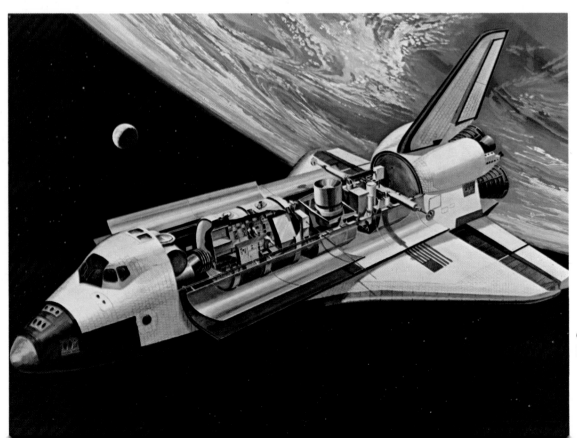

Spacelab and
Columbia showing
how the two fit together.

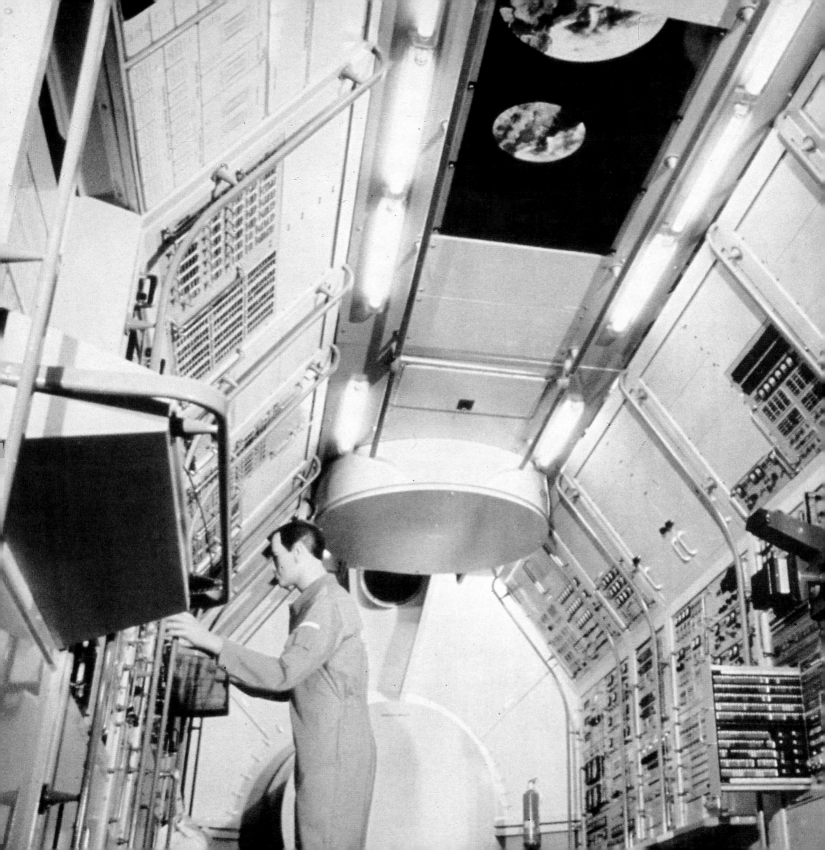

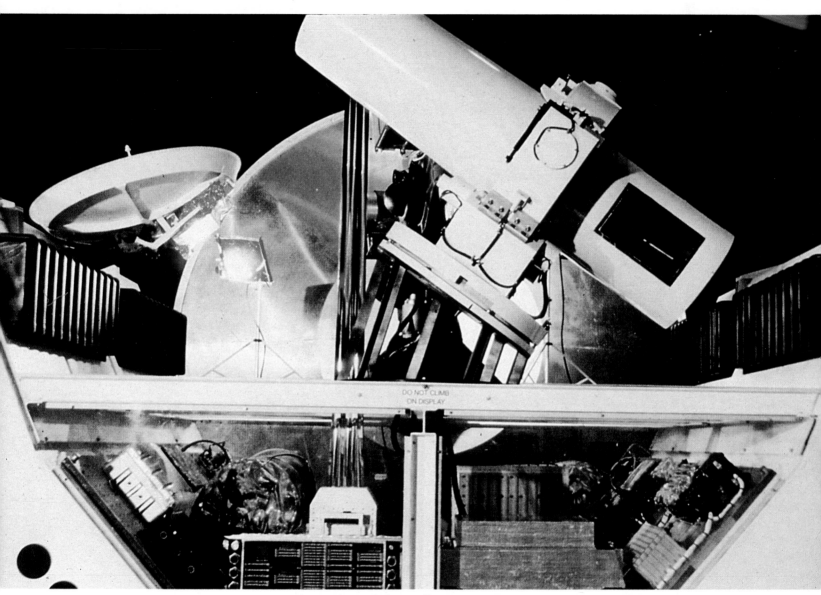

A portion of the pallet section of ESA's Spacelab. (The pressurized portion is in the background.) The main instrument is the ultraviolet telescope. Beneath it are controls, power supply, recorders, and communication equipment.

Columbia with cargo-bay doors open. Spacelab cameras and measuring instruments point toward Earth. They photograph cloud cover, forested regions, ocean shallows and currents; measure heat radiation, magnetic fields, light absorption.

Apollo and Soyuz rendezvous in space. This mission emphasized that space is international.

An Earth station receives microwaves from the solar collector. The electricity is changed to the kind we use in our homes and then sent out to cities and towns.

The first colonies in space will appear like huge wheels (tires) with six spokes that connect to the hub. Mirrors "floating" in space direct sunlight to controlled areas in the colony. Space factories are located at the end of long transport tubes.

A residential area inside the tire of a colony. Life in a space colony is not that much different from life on Earth.

4.

From 1957 to Columbia

Some people believe that the space age began with the first flight of the space shuttle. Perhaps so. Certainly that flight started the era of space use, the time when we began to use space wisely rather than just explore it. Others, however, say that the space age began a quarter of a century earlier when the first satellite was put into orbit around the Earth. That was October 4, 1957, when the Russians launched Sputnik, a small satellite that excited the whole world.

Sputnik also challenged scientists and engineers in the United States. Three months later the challenge was met. On January 31, 1958, Explorer 1 was launched into space. It was the first American satellite.

Edwin Aldrin on the moon. The landing vehicle and Neil
Armstrong, who took this picture, can be seen reflected from
Aldrin's visor. This was a major step toward the space shuttle.

From that time on, there was feverish activity as both countries continued to explore space. Various sorts of satellites were built and launched by both the Soviet Union and the United States. They contained instruments that measured and recorded space conditions, and relayed the information back to Earth.

The next big step came in 1961. On April 12, the Russians sent Uri Gagarin into space. He traveled once around the Earth—Gagarin was the first space traveler. That mission started a series of manned expeditions into space. In the United States there was the Mercury series of flights (one man), and the Gemini series (two men). In the Soviet Union there was the Vostok series and the Voskhod series. On a flight that began on June 16, 1963, Valentina Tereshkova, the first woman to go into orbit, made forty-eight journeys around the Earth.

But the achievement that shook the world, and which was seen live on television by a large part of it, came at 10:56:20 (EDT) in the evening of July 20, 1969. At that moment Neil Armstrong, the American astronaut, stepped onto the surface of the moon—man had walked on another world.

A new dimension of discovery opened up. People could leave planet Earth and land elsewhere in the solar system. Maybe they could even land on Mars, or make long voyages beyond the solar system. Perhaps they could live in space colonies. First, however, answers had to be found to many important questions. Could people survive in space over long periods of time? Could they work in space? Was it possible for humans to use space?

We found answers to these questions in 1973 when Skylab was launched. Crews aboard this gigantic vehicle—it was 36 meters long and weighed 76 tons—remained aboard for three months. They suffered no serious effects. There were many problems, however. One of the more important concerned exercise. The crew's routine required them to use their muscles, but because there is zero gravity in space, a person moves with very little effort; muscles tended to go soft in spite of the exercise. There were also problems concerning the blood's supply of sodium and potassium. On Earth, gravity tends to pull blood down toward a person's feet. But this does not happen in zero gravity. The blood is more evenly distributed throughout the body. The body reacts as though there were a sudden increase in the amount of blood. In trying to correct this situation, the body gives off fluids by perspiring and excreting more urine.

This causes body weight to drop. Also, it causes a drop in sodium and potassium, two of the many substances that are in the excreted liquids—urine, for the most part. Over a period of a few hours, the body corrects the sodium lack by gradually retaining more fluids. But potassium continues to be lost. This makes it impossible for the muscles to function properly. The decrease in muscle activity may, in severe cases, affect the heart muscles, producing uneven heart action.

After a few hours, and sometimes as long as a day or so, the body adjusts to the changes. Breathing speeds up and gradually the kidneys begin to retain more of the potassium. A new balance is established, body weight and blood volume even off at the best levels for the weightless condition.

Another, and quite different kind of problem occurred when Skylab was launched. One of the solar panels—flat surfaces covered with solar-electric cells—failed to open. This meant there would be insufficient electricity for the equipment. Also, the heat shield that protected the inside of the ship from the intense heat of the sun ripped off. It was feared that the entire mission would fail. After much study by engineers, a plan was worked out to correct the problems. The crew flew up to Skylab, their ship docked, and the crew transferred to the lab. Following the plan developed on Earth, they spent hours working to release the solar panel. They also erected a thin plastic canopy over the lab to protect it from the hot sunshine. This showed that people can work in space, but it is not easy. For example, it is hard to lift things in space, for there may be no foothold for leverage. When you lift something on Earth, your feet push down on the ground, or the floor. There's nothing like that in space. You don't lift; you just hold on to whatever you want to move. Then you must pull yourself and the load by using a handhold or a line of some sort. Movement is also difficult. Astronauts move in space by releasing short bursts from small jet engines that are fastened to their space suits. But movements must be made carefully, or the astronauts could go into an uncontrolled spin without moving anywhere, or they could accidentally shoot themselves away from the ship. This could be disastrous, for in space movements do not stop. Once an object is in motion, it can move forever. There is nothing to stop it. So the astronauts always have a tether fastened to them, a line that holds them to the ship. It is also difficult to use tools in space. When using a wrench, for example, the astronauts are just as apt to turn themselves as they are the nuts or bolts that are being tightened. They must hold on to the ship to keep from spinning about. Even though there were many such difficulties, repairs to Skylab were made. It was a fine example of the way people can work in space and cope with emergencies, even though the effort is extremely tiring.

There have been three flights to Skylab. One crew remained aboard for three months. Later on, the Russians sent cosmonauts to a similar station of their own, and they spent a hundred and forty days there. Humans can certainly work in space, and they can live there for long periods of time. Skylab was abandoned and left in orbit after the third mission. There is an illustration of Skylab on pages 62 and 63.

While the United States was developing Apollo, the vehicle that carried astronauts to the moon and to Skylab, the Russians were developing a similar ship called Soyuz. Two years after Skylab was launched, an Apollo ship and a Soyuz

Cutaway of Skylab is at the right. It was as long as five cars, bumper to bumper. The Apollo vehicle that carried the crew from Earth, and returned them, is at the left. At top center are the solar panels that generate electricity for the space telescope just above the panels.

hooked together in space. A color illustration of that rendezvous appears on page 54. The Russians and Americans moved from one ship to the other. This was a big achievement, for it showed that ships could rendezvous successfully, and that space exploration is truly an international undertaking. Its benefits affect all people, no matter where on Earth they may live.

During the 1960's and 1970's, space launchers were developed, people learned how to live in space, and much was learned about space conditions and the hazards that might develop. As the 1970's came to a close, we were ready to use space. Before that could be done, however, there had to be ways of reducing costs.

No longer could we afford to send a ship into space and then just throw it away. The world was ready for the space shuttle.

Science had come a long way in a short time. The first successful flight of a powered airplane was made less than a hundred years ago. In a few decades, airplanes grew into supersonic transports (SST's) and into huge liners that carry five-hundred passengers; and rockets became powerful enough to make flights to the moon.

5.

From Space Shuttle to Space Base to Space Colony

One of the main tasks of Columbia was to carry Spacelab, which tested many ways that industry can use space. The cost of the mission has been met by the people; their governments and their taxes have paid for it. But this will be changed by the shuttle program, and the projects it will make possible. The value of electricity and goods made in space will pay a large part of the future bills. Private industry of many nations will build their own space factories and energy collectors. They will sell space-made products to consumers in all parts of the world. Industries will use space shuttles to ferry materials and workers back and forth between Earth and the space installations.

65

A typical space factory. It is completely automatic, operated on command from space-control center on Earth. Panels of solar cells generate electricity. A space shuttle is moving in to deposit raw materials, and pick up finished products.

SPACE BASE FOR MANUFACTURING

In the next few years shuttles will set up factories that will make a variety of products. A factory will be made on Earth. Then it will be taken apart, and the pieces of it will be carried into space by several shuttles. Once in orbit, the pieces will be unloaded. They will be tied together to keep them from floating away as they are removed from the cargo bay. The pieces will remain in orbit. Engineers in space suits will then put the pieces together. The shuttles will make quick returns to Earth for additional parts of the factory.

One of the products made in space factories will be perfect crystals. Crystals are particular arrangements of atoms. If you put a lot of salt in water, crystals of salt will grow in the solution. And the atoms that make the salt will always be arranged in the same pattern. Salt has little use as crystals, but crystals of various other materials, quartz for example, are used widely in electronics of all kinds to control and conduct electric currents. But their usefulness is limited because here on Earth crystals are not pure; they may have small cracks in them, or the molecules of which they are made may be slightly out of line. These imperfections affect the electricity in an unpredictable manner as it goes through the crystal, or they may cause unwanted vibrations of the crystal. Crystals that are perfect can be grown in space. There is nothing there to pollute the crystal, not even the container. The solution in which the crystals grow does not need a container. The liquid remains suspended in space. Since there is zero gravity, there is no force to pull it down. Also, in zero gravity, the material is evenly distributed, making the crystal the same throughout. These crystals will enable engineers to produce extremely accurate parts for computers. They will also make possible reliable and long-lasting microcircuits which are very small electric switches and controls, for use in medical devices that regulate heart rhythm, and keep track of circulation, breathing, and other body functions.

67

A typical space factory is shown in the illustration on page 66. This is a crystal factory. No people are needed to run it; it is controlled by radio from a central station on Earth. Power is supplied by panels of solar cells that can be seen on either side of the factory. The cells change sunlight into electricity. An orbiter is shown moving in toward the factory. The cargo handler holds a supply of raw materials that will be eased into place. Once this is done, the handler will pick up the completed crystals and store them in the cargo bay for return to Earth.

Metal processing is another important use for space factories. In space, metals can be melted outside of a container. There is no gravity or any other force to move the metal. So, just as solid metal can float free in space, so can liquid metal. This means that, like crystals, metals can be kept free of pollution. Also, in space, materials of different densities will combine—something they will not readily do on Earth. For example, liquid glass and steel can be mixed together in space; they blend together because gravity on both is the same—it is zero. And, by blowing gases into melted metals and making a sort of froth, unheard-of materials can be produced. Steel as light as a feather, but with the strength of ordinary steel can be made. Ball bearings perfectly round and exactly the same throughout can be manufactured. Much of the wear on ball bearings made on Earth is caused by slight variations in roundness. Since the space bearings will be perfect, they will probably last forever, there will be so little wear.

Glass that is perfect can also be made in space. There would be nothing to pollute the melted glass. It is believed that this perfect glass will result in lenses that will greatly improve results obtained with cameras, microscopes, telescopes—anything that uses lenses.

Magnets made in space are much stronger and longer lasting than those made on Earth. A metal becomes magnetic when the molecules are lined up in a regular order, rather than being arranged in a random fashion. In space this lining up is more perfect, so the magnet is more powerful. Such magnets will make electric motors more efficient, since they will run on less electricity. All other devices that use magnets will also work better.

Other space factories will be devoted to medical research and the biological sciences. Certain drugs used to treat diseases can be made better and more cheaply in zero gravity than on Earth. In zero gravity, substances do not settle. (For example, if on Earth you put some soil into water, the soil will settle, with the heaviest particles on the bottom. In space the soil would never settle—there is no downward pull.) This non-settling condition is needed in the processing of certain materials from which medicines are made.

Scientists are hopeful that in zero gravity it may be possible to make substances that cannot be made on Earth. An example might be a compound to take the place of insulin, which is now used by diabetics. Insulin is a substance produced by the pancreas. A person who does not have enough insulin is diabetic. The patient is treated by receiving insulin shots. The only way of getting the insulin is from the pancreas organs of slaughtered animals. Many people are distressed by insulin because of allergies associated with the animals. Also, the cost of insulin is high because of the limited supply.

Tests indicate that under the high vacuum and zero gravity of space, it may be possible to manufacture insulin in large quantities, and from materials that have nothing to do with animals. It will be absolutely free of pollutants. Diabetics would have a plentiful supply, and at a reasonable price.

These are just a few of the possible uses of space factories. No doubt, as factories are developed, there will be hundreds of products that they can make—and some of them we have not even dreamed about.

SPACE BASE FOR ENERGY

The oil, gas, and coal we use today were formed millions of years ago. Some of it goes back 300 million years to the Paleozoic era. Eventually all the deposits of these fossil fuels will be used up. At the same time demands for energy will become greater because there will be more people in the world—more cars, airplanes, and factories—and everyone will be enjoying a higher standard of living.

One way of producing energy to reduce the drain on fossil fuels and yet meet the growing needs is by using nuclear energy. At the present time over two hundred nuclear plants are operating in a dozen countries around the world. And more of them are being built.

Nuclear fuels may eventually replace fossil fuels as our main source of energy. If they do not, engineers must turn to other sources. The one that is most plentiful and longest lasting is the sun, which gives us solar energy. Earth-based solar-energy collectors are now operating around the world. But there are many problems. Massive, expensive installations are needed to produce useful amounts of electricity. Also, solar collectors do not work too well in cold climates; they do not work at all at night or on cloudy days.

Solar-energy collectors in space would solve many of these problems. The idea may seem a fantasy, but such structures can be put together, and building them is a logical chore for future space shuttles.

The solar collector will be panels of several thousand solar cells fastened together. The entire collector will be about 35 000 kilometers away from Earth, and it will stay above the same part of Earth at all times. Sunlight will fall upon it twenty-four hours a day. Weather conditions on Earth will have no effect on its operation.

On Earth there will be a receiving station directly beneath the solar collector, as shown in the illustration on page 55.

A Satellite Solar Power Station (SSPS) is a huge array of solar cells. They convert solar energy into electricity. Microwaves transmit the electricity to collecting stations on Earth.

Electricity produced in the satellite will be changed to very short wave electricity—microwaves. In this form the electricity can be beamed to Earth, much as television signals are beamed from satellites. At the receiving station the micro-beam will be changed to ordinary electricity and fed into wires that will carry it to cities and towns. The beam will be about seven kilometers wide when it arrives on Earth. The antenna picking up the microwaves will be that wide. It will be fenced in to keep people away, for the energy in the beam can be harmful. Just outside the fence there will be no hazard, for the energy level will be about the same as the energy from a microwave oven when the door is closed.

The satellite power station will be some 48 square kilometers in area. It will be built in space, the parts taken to the location aboard space shuttles. Once constructed, engines will be fastened to it. They will push the station farther out, putting it into an orbit that will take it once around the Earth as Earth turns once around. This is called a geosynchronous orbit, an orbit that matches Earth's rotation. The engines will push the station slowly, taking several months to get it into position.

Electricity from the collector will of course be free from chemical pollution, as is all electricity. Since no fuel will be burned to produce it, there will be no pollution from that source, and very little of the electricity will be lost as heat to the atmosphere—another kind of pollution. One power station could produce five gigawatts of power. (In metric, giga means one billion.) It could produce this electricity all the time, both day and night. Five gigawatts is three times the amount of electricity produced by the Grand Coulee dam electric-generating station. It is enough electricity to fill the needs of the city of Los Angeles and also of the area for miles around.

One plan calls for 180 of these power stations to be strung across the sky by the twenty-first century. The stations could supply one quarter of all the electricity needed in the United States. Similar arrays at other locations could furnish electricity for other parts of the world—Europe, Asia, Africa, and Australia.

SPACE BASE FOR COMMUNICATION

Through the centuries, letter writing has not changed very much. One must still write the letter, put it into an envelope, seal it, and deliver it to the post office. Then the long process begins of canceling the stamps, sorting, bagging, picking up, transporting, sorting, delivering. There is a better way—space mail.

Letters will be sent from station to station electrically by using a mail satellite. The message will be sent to a satellite on a radio wave, relayed from there to a receiving station where the letter will be printed out and then delivered. Or the letter may be a direct copy of the original; it would look exactly the same. All this will be done with privacy, just as there is privacy when you talk on a telephone. Delivery of the mail will be faster, more reliable, and much less expensive.

Equipment for space mail will be an antenna about 300 meters across, made on Earth and then assembled some 500 kilometers above the Earth. The platform for the antenna will be made from metal pipes and joints that will be numbered and keyed. All the parts needed could be carried into space by three space shuttles. Once there, the parts will be put together. It is expected that the antenna can be finished less than a year after the project is started.

A single antenna could handle thousands of letters at the same time. With a system of antennas located around the globe it will be possible to send a communication to almost anyone in the world, and to do so within an hour.

An antenna array for space-mail. Signals are picked up from Earth and redirected to receivers at a distant location. At lower center a shuttle is moving in to service the antenna.

SPACE TELEPHONES

People on Earth can communicate easily by citizens' band radio. But the range is limited, and conversations are public.

Telephone antennas that are carried into space, constructed and serviced by shuttle, will make it possible for people to communicate privately, no matter where they may be. A call to Europe, or to Asia, or to the corner store, may be transmitted by satellite. At the present time commercial satellites relay telephone messages over long distances, but the service is limited and the cost is much higher than it would be with a large space transmitter.

A typical space array needed for this service will be made of three antenna "dishes," each about 26 meters across. These dishes will pick up messages from Earth and transmit them to the receiver. Power to operate the equipment will come from a large solar-cell panel, some 75 meters long and wide, and weighing 15 tons or so. Solar cells mounted on the panel will convert solar energy to electricity, a never-ending and practically maintenance-free source of power. One satellite could easily handle messages for three million users. A system of them would be needed for worldwide coverage.

Cost of operation would be lower than present relay satellites, mainly because the space equipment is long-lasting and much easier to maintain. The lower costs would make for wider usage. Information could be obtained from anywhere in the world. At the present time a person in Europe, for example, can call an information bank in Washington and get immediate answers to his questions. But the service is costly. With wide use of space telephones, the cost will be much lower and the service immediate. Doctors in one part of the world will be able to give directions to other doctors who might be faced with an emergency on some other continent. Communication will be direct, person-to-person, without the use of central switching stations, and the voices will be loud and clear between people anywhere on Earth. A first step in developing space-telephoning will be to experiment with antennas fastened to an orbiter. Once the system is workable, the money earned by it will pay the expenses. In fact, industry will very likely also pay a large part of the development costs.

SPACE COLONIES

Some day, perhaps as early as the first part of the next century, shuttles will be involved in the building of a space colony. Materials for the colony will be carried into space by dozens of shuttle flights. Engineers and mechanics housed in a shuttle will assemble the parts in space. Life-support equipment—air, water, and food—will be provided by Earth until the space colony is operating; until it has become self-sufficient.

Very likely, most of the materials needed will eventually come not from Earth, but from the moon. A group of technicians in a settlement on the moon will mine the surface, and send lunar ore to a processing station in space. Here metals will be extracted from the ores, processed into steel beams, tubes, and pipes and be used to build the space colony.

Present planners, engineers from the National Aeronautics and Space Agency (NASA) and from the American Society of Engineers' education division, have studied several different designs for the space colony. They see the most likely design as a tube 130 meters in diameter. The tube is curved into a wheel, like a bicycle tire. The wheel is large, almost 1.8 kilometers in diameter. Ten thousand people will live in the colony. They will live inside the "tire." It is connected by six large, straight tubes (spokes) to a central station—the hub of the wheel. Spacecraft from Earth, from other colonies, and from space factories will dock at the hub.

The spokes of the wheel are hollow. They will contain transport cars for moving people and cargo to and from the

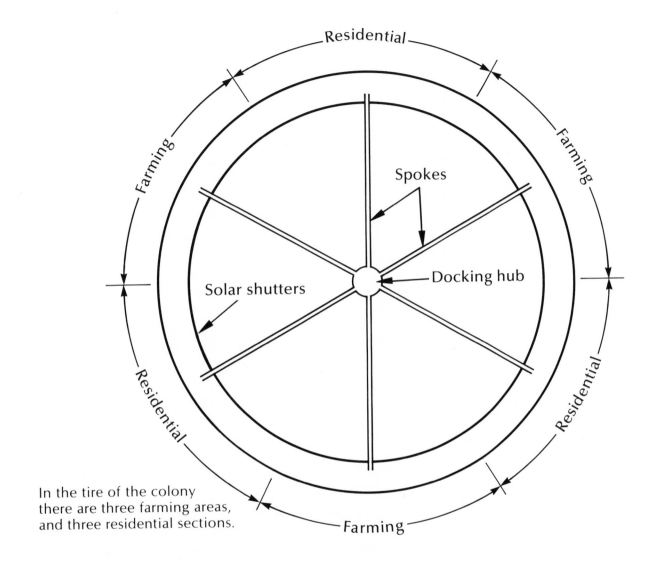

Residential

Farming

Spokes

Docking hub

Solar shutters

Residential

Residential

Farming

Residential

In the tire of the colony
there are three farming areas,
and three residential sections.

Farming

hub to the wheel itself. Three of the six spokes go to residence
areas in the tube; the other three go to farming areas.

The entire wheel is turning, making one revolution a min-
ute and moving about 9 kilometers an hour. This turning
makes an artificial gravity, much the same as the "gravity" that
holds water in a pail when you swing it over your head at

arm's length. "Down" will be away from the center of the wheel. In the "tire" portion, one would experience all effects due to gravity, down and up, for example, just as one experiences them on Earth. As one moved toward the hub, gravity would become less, reaching zero at the hub. People will live along the outer rim in terraced apartments that are placed among trees and flowers.

About half of the tire is to be used for farming. Agricultural engineers will carefully control the chemicals in the soil (which will come from the moon), and the water supply (recycled at all times) to produce the greatest amount of crops in the least amount of space. Hydrogen for the water will come from Earth and oxygen from lunar rocks.

Above the hub there will be a large mirror angled toward the sun. It will be motionless in space, not spinning with the colony. Sunlight will reflect from the mirror to rings of smaller mirrors that surround the hub. These mirrors will direct the sunlight into the tube. Automatic shutters in the tube will control the sunlight, reduce it as temperature rises, or shut it out completely. Every twelve hours the shutters will close to produce the day-night sequence. Closer in toward the hub, solar-cell panels will produce electricity for the colony.

Extending from the hub at a right angle to the spokes (somewhat like the axle of a wheel) will be a transport tube about 10 kilometers long. At the end of the tube will be a space factory. A typical space factory might contain a solar furnace that develops a temperature of several thousand degrees. The high temperature is used to refine metals. Pure metals are then combined with glass and other materials, as mentioned earlier, to make light but strong parts for machines and construction.

The first colony will be located 380 000 kilometers from Earth, about the same distance as the moon. It will move almost in the moon's orbit, but will trail the moon by about 200 000 kilometers. This location will assure that the colony

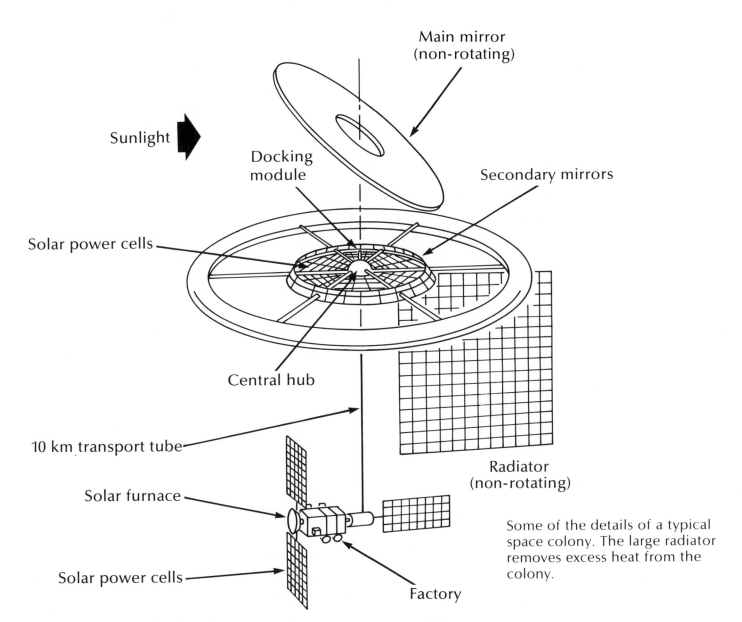

Main mirror
(non-rotating)

Sunlight

Docking
module

Secondary mirrors

Solar power cells

Central hub

10 km transport tube

Radiator
(non-rotating)

Solar furnace

Solar power cells

Factory

Some of the details of a typical space colony. The large radiator removes excess heat from the colony.

will always be in sunlight, even during infrequent eclipses. Also, the location will make it fairly easy to send ships to the moon, and to receive materials from lunar collecting stations.

In many ways life in the colony will be very much like life on Earth. There will be no awareness of being in space; no feeling of motion of the station, and of course there will be

79

gravity of sorts that will give the feeling of up and down. When people look up they will see blue. It will look like Earth's sky, but in fact it will be tinted blinds. At night when the shutters are closed, the "sky" will be dull, with no stars at all, unless some way is worked out to produce an artificial star-filled sky. There will be trees, flowers, and birds. A person will be busy, for there will be playgrounds, movies, swimming pools, shopping areas, and schools and libraries. When a family wishes to go on vacation, they might rent a space wagon. This will be a jet-powered vehicle garaged in the hub. People will board it; then it will go through a hatch and into outer space. A vacation might be a jaunt to the moon station. Or it might simply be a journey out and around the space colony, seeing it all at once from the outside, as space observers. And at the same time they would see the stars bright, sharp and clear as they can never be seen from Earth. Eventually, a vacation might include trips to other colonies at different locations.

Inside the colony the air will be like our air here on Earth except that it will be much cleaner. There will be no pollution, for there will be no factories producing chemical waste products (factories are outside the colony); no fuels will be burned, so there will be no smoke or fuel wastes, and no insecticides will be needed.

People will walk to get about in the living areas. Some will have bicycles, but these will be more for exercise than for transportation. To get around more quickly there will be small electric cars that are public and so used by everyone as needed. These will run on an overhead rail ("overhead" is toward the hub of the wheel). People will use them when they want to get from one living area to another, or from one of the farm sections to another one. It will be a lot simpler than going all the way to the hub inside one of the spokes, getting into zero gravity, which will cause some people to become nauseous, and moving out again.

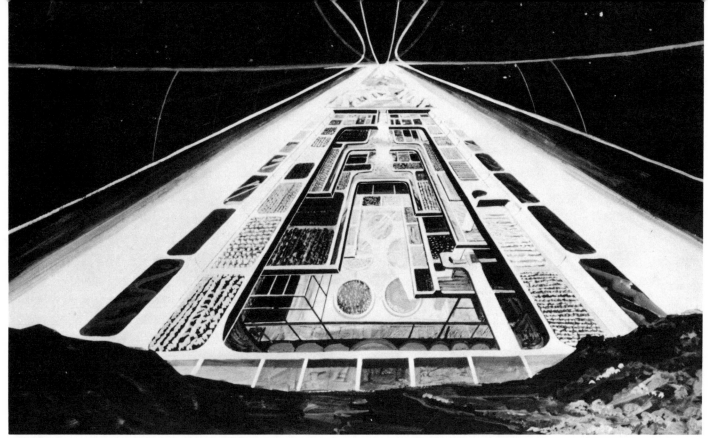

The agricultural area of a space colony. Crops are supplied with water from the river in the foreground and also from the fish tanks that line the sides.

Long ago people dreamed about living in space. And some of the space pioneers like Robert Goddard in the United States and Konstantin Tsiolkovsky in the Soviet Union made rough designs for a space colony. But the idea for the colony discussed here is new. It began about the same time that people were developing the space shuttle. The whole idea of living in space was fantastic and it still is to a lot of people. But the space colony is a solid idea, and one that the space shuttle will help to make a reality. Engineers will learn a lot from the first colony, and that knowledge will help them design even larger colonies. Eventually space colonies may be large enough to hold a population of a hundred thousand people, and maybe even more. One day you or your children may be living in a space colony—the frontier of the twenty-first century.

After a successful first mission, the space shuttle Columbia gently returns to Earth at Edwards Air Force Base.

Major Strides in Space

1957 – *October 4*—Sputnik, first satellite to go around Earth.

1960 – *August 12*—Echo 1, first satellite to transmit television.

1960 – *August 19, 20*—First animals (Belka and Strelka) recovered from space: two dogs that made eighteen orbits in Sputnik 5.

1961 – *April 12*—Yuri A. Gagarin, first man in space, made one orbit in Vostok 1.

82

1962 – *August 11, 15*—First double-launch of manned spacecraft.

1963 – *June 16–19*—Valentina V. Tereshkova, first woman in space, made forty-eight orbits in Vostok 6.

1965 – *March 18*—Alexei A. Leonov made the first spacewalk: 20 minutes outside of Voskhod 2.

1965 – *June 28*—Early Bird, launched April 6, 1965, is the first commercial communication satellite to link U.S. and Europe.

1966 – *February 3*—Luna 9 makes the first unmanned soft landing on the Moon; first photos of lunar surface.

1966 – *March 1*—Venera 3, launched Nov. 16, 1965, is the first man-made object to land on another planet: the surface of Venus.

1966 – *May 30*—Surveyor 1 takes first U.S. pictures on lunar surface.

1967 – *October 18*—Venera 4 makes first transmission of information about atmosphere of Venus during 90-minute descent.

1968 – *December*—Apollo 8 makes first manned orbit of the Moon.

1969 – *July*—Mariner 6 makes first low pass over Mars: altitude, only 3431 kilometers.

1969 – *July 20*—Neil A. Armstrong is the first man to set foot on another world: Moon landing of Apollo 11.

1969 – *October*—Seven cosmonauts in orbit at the same time: triple launching of Soyuz 6, 7, and 8.

1970 – *September*—First unmanned Moon landing that also returned soil samples to Earth, Luna 16.

1970 – *November 17*—First use of unmanned vehicle on the Moon: Lunokhod 1, commanded from Earth, completed program Nov. 22, 1970, went 197 meters.

1971 – *April 19*—Salyut 1, first space station in orbit, occupied on June 7 after rendezvous with Soyuz 11.

1971—*July, August*—Lunar rover, first vehicle to carry astronauts on Moon surface, travels 27 kilometers, Apollo 15.

1971—*November 27*—First space capsule lands on Mars, ejected by Mars 2.

1973—*December 3*—Pioneer 10 makes first space investigation of Jupiter from distance of 130 000 kilometers.

1974—*November 16-February 8*—Space-flight endurance record of 84 days set by Skylab crew. (In 1978 the Russians spent 140 days in orbit aboard their space station.)

1974—*March 23-April 5*—Mariner 10 makes first spacecraft investigation of Mercury; one spacecraft subsequently encountered Venus once and Mercury three times.

1975—*July 15-24*—Apollo-Soyuz Test Project (ASTP), first international-manned space flight.

1976—*July 20*—Vikings 1 and 2 make first long-period mission on surface of Mars; sample soil, take pictures, search for life.

1981—*April 12*—Columbia goes into orbit on first test flight. Age of space shuttle or STS (Space Transport System) begins. Mission lasted two days, six hours.

1982—*November 11*—Columbia's first working mission launches two communications satellites. Four-man crew is in orbit five days.

1983—*April 4*—Challenger, Columbia's sister ship, is launched. Releases Tracking and Data Relay satellite (TDRS). Carries heaviest of all payloads.

1983—*June 18*—Challenger carries five-person crew, including Sally K. Ride, first American woman to go into space.

1983—*November 28*—Columbia begins sixth flight and carries Spacelab into orbit. Six-man crew conducts scores of experiments for industry and medicine; and ways to control motion sickness.

Index